The History of God's World

Written by R. Meredith Emery

Illustrated by Nikola Belley

The History of God's World
Copyright © 2018 by R. Meredith Emery
Publisher: By His Grace Publishing.
All rights reserved. No part of this book may be reproduced or copied in any form without written permission from the author.
Illustrations: Nikola Belley
Printed in the United States of America
ISBN: 978-0-9991835-2-6

Dedicated to the women and men who
lived before me that I, too, might live,
especially to my mama, Irene,
and my daddy, Russell.

With gratitude to those
who have patiently taught
God's Word to me through the years,
especially Major Ian W. Thomas.

A special thank you
to my husband whose life has
testified of Christ to me.

Written for my precious children -
Elizabeth, Samuel, Daniel, and Paul
and for those who come
beside you and after you.

May you believe the truth about your
Creator, His World and
His Everlasting Love for you!

Foreword

The History of God's World is a non-denominational, theological narrative for children beginning with Creation and continuing through to the New Earth. It is not a Bible "Storybook". Instead, it is a framework on which young believers may add future Bible study while believing the following Bible truths.

God created the world and everything in it. It belongs to Him.

We are made in the image of God with a body, soul, and spirit.

We were created to live forever with God. Death came only through sin.

God knows what will give His children the greatest joy and what will hurt us.

Man and woman first sinned when they chose to decide for themselves what was good and what was evil instead of believing and obeying God.

Since the first sin, all people have sinned and live in bodies that will die.

Jesus is the image of the invisible God. He left heaven to rescue His people from death.

God sees us as perfect and holy when by His grace, we turn from sin, believe Jesus died and was buried as the propitiation for our sin, and God raised Him from the dead to live forever.

With belief in the finished work of Jesus comes the gift of the Holy Spirit to live in us and bring our dead souls to life.

Someday, God will give new bodies to His children, and we will live forever with Him in a new and perfect world.

The Beginning

In the beginning, before there was a world,
God was already there.
We cannot understand everything about God
because He is so wonderful, but we know
He can do anything.
He knows everything,
and He is everywhere all of the time.

God spoke His all-powerful Word and created the world and every star in the universe. It all belonged to Him. It was beautiful and perfect. It was so perfect that if you knew where to look, you could see pictures of God in everything He made.

God wanted children who were also pictures of Him, so He shaped a man out of the dust. He gave the man a body that could move and work and play. He gave him a soul which could think and reason and love. And *God gave the man His Spirit* so he could understand the ways of his Creator.

God loved His new child and walked with him showing him all that He had made. The man loved and trusted his Father to take care of him and to give him every good thing.

God planted a beautiful garden where the man could live. In the middle of the garden, He planted two special trees. The fruit of the one tree would let the man live forever. Its name was - The Tree of Life. The name of the other tree was - The Tree of Knowing What Is Good and What Is Evil. *That tree belonged only to God.*

Since God had created man, He was the only one who knew what would make him happy and what would hurt him. Man could eat from the Tree of Life, but God warned him that eating fruit from the other tree would cause him to die.

All of God's animals were made to be male and female so they could have babies, but the man was all alone. So God made a beautiful woman to be the man's friend and helper. He told the man and the woman to take care of the world and fill it with children.

The Lie

Everything was just the way God wanted it to be. He was filled with joy to see His children loving each other in the beautiful world He had made. But God had an evil enemy. We call him Satan. Long ago, Satan had been a beautiful angel in Heaven. But he became jealous of God and wanted *to be God*, so he had to leave Heaven.

Now, Satan wanted to destroy all that God had created. So he came to the woman disguised as one of God's beautiful creatures. He told the woman that the fruit from God's Tree was *good* to eat and would *not* make her die. He said it would make her smart enough to make her own decisions and not *need* God.

The woman wasn't sure if she could believe what God had said about the tree. The fruit *looked* good to eat. So, the woman decided to believe Satan and eat from God's Tree. Then she gave some of the fruit to the man and he chose to eat from it, too. That day, God's children decided for themselves what was right and what was wrong instead of trusting and obeying God.

This was the first sin in God's beautiful world, and *that sin changed everything*. The lives of the man and the woman were now broken. Their bodies and their minds were still working for they had been wonderfully made by God, but something had happened to their spirits! For the first time, they knew they were naked. Now, instead of looking forward to seeing God in the garden, they tried to hide from Him because they were ashamed of what they had done.

God had given the man and the woman the freedom to choose. Even though they had chosen to disobey, God still loved them. But now, their lives would have pain and sadness. And the world would no longer be as perfect as God had designed it to be.

God promised His children that He would someday crush the one who had tempted them. Then, He did something that made His children very sad. It made God sad, too, as He took the skin from one of His beautiful animals and used it to cover the nakedness of the man and the woman. They had never seen blood before and the animal was not moving. It frightened them! They began to understand some of the horrible consequences of their sin.

God wanted His children to live forever but not in a broken world. The man and the woman would have to leave the beautiful place where the Tree of Life grew, and where they had walked and talked with their Father. Now, instead of living forever, those beautiful bodies that God had created would turn back into dust, the same dust that God had used to make Adam. But the worst consequence of their sin was what happened inside of them. The Spirit of Life had left them. And without God's Spirit, they were now dead inside.

The Broken World

And so, the man and the woman began their lives outside of the garden and away from God. How sorry they must have been that they had not believed and obeyed their Creator. How confused they must have become when God was not always there to tell them what was good for them and what would hurt them. And how alone they must have felt without their Father.

Now, God named the man Adam which means "red earth" because the man had been created out of the dust of the earth. And Adam named the woman Eve which means "Life" because she would be the mother of many children.

Soon, people began to fill up the world, but they were all born without God's Spirit alive in them. Without God's Spirit, they were not able to understand the ways of God. They did not honor Him as their Creator or thank Him for His goodness to them. They became selfish and jealous. They fought, and even killed one another.

God's heart grew sad when He saw how violent and evil the people had become. He decided to wash away all of the evil in His world with a flood of water and *begin all over again!*

God chose a man named Noah to be a part of His new beginning. He gave Noah instructions to build a ship. It was to be so large that Noah, his family, and many animals could live on it for a long time. When the ship was finished, God caused water to come from above the world and water to come up out of the ground until the whole world was covered with deep water. Noah, his family, and the animals stayed on the ship until the water dried up.

Many things were different after the flood of water, but it was still God's wonderful world. God promised He would never flood the whole world again. He told Noah and his family to go out and fill the world with children just as He had told Adam and Eve so many years before. It was a new and good beginning, but it did not save the people from the consequences of sin.

The Special Family

God had not forgotten His promise to rescue the people from sin and death. He had always had a plan to send His Son to the world to be their Rescuer. But when His Son came to the world, He would need a family for God had always chosen for His children to live in families. And this family would need to understand the ways of God.

God chose a man to be the father of this special family and named him Abraham which means "the father of many." He gave Abraham his own land where he and his family could live. And He told Abraham that his family would become like the stars of the sky - so many that they could not even be counted. He promised that all of the world would be blessed by Abraham's family and Abraham believed all that God said.

And so, this family began to grow. They became different from the other people of the world, and God began to show Himself to the world through them. And in time, God would send His Son into this family to rescue the people from all the sorrow that sin had caused.

God is love and everything He does comes from His love. All love comes from Him, and there would be no love without Him.

God's children were created to be like God. So God gave His special family a gift. It was a gift that would help them live the way they had been created to live - loving God and loving one another.

God wrote down what love would do and what love would not do and gave these rules to His people to keep forever. This gift would help Abraham's family get ready to welcome the one who would rescue them.

The people tried to obey these rules of love, but sometimes they chose to decide for themselves which ones were good and which were not. Their wrong choices always brought sad consequences for no one could ever choose a better way than the one who had created them.

God did not stop loving His people when they disobeyed, but their sin made Him sad. It even made Him angry, because God wanted His people to be filled with joy and just as wonderful as He had created them to be. He knew that sin would only bring sadness and death to them.

The people needed more than rules to obey. They needed God's Spirit to be alive in them as He had been in the beginning.

God did many wonderful things in the lives of those who believed Him and obeyed Him. His Spirit was with them, and He did mighty miracles in their lives. Some of God's people had children even when they were very old. God raised some of them up to become mighty rulers and leaders. The people were saved from their enemies and won wars. Some who were weak were made strong. God protected others from lions and bears. Some even saw their dead loved ones come back to life.

God's children kept watching and waiting for the one God had promised to send - the one who would be their Rescuer. People in other lands began to see that this family belonged to the one, true and mighty God. This was part of God's plan because He wanted people all over His wonderful world to be rescued from sin and death.

The Promised One

When the time was right, God the Father sent God the Son from the wonderful place we call Heaven to live with this special family. The Son was the image of the invisible God and had come to rescue the people just as God had promised so many years before.

But God's Son did not come as a man, strong and powerful. He came as a baby. His name was Jesus which means, The Lord Saves, for in Him God had truly come to save His people.

Jesus lived with his mother, Mary, and her husband, Joseph. They lived in Israel which was the same land God had given to Abraham and his family so many years before. Even though God was Jesus' real father, Joseph took care of Jesus just like any loving father would. And Jesus lived and grew just as any boy would – except for one thing. Jesus never decided for himself what was good and what was evil. Instead, He always obeyed His Father.

Jesus was the first man since Adam who was just as God intended man to be - complete, with God's Spirit living inside Him. When the time was right, Jesus left his home and went out into the land of Israel to do all the things God had planned for him to do. He began by being baptized.

Jesus walked and talked with God's most special creation, His beloved people. He taught the people about God's great love for them. He healed the sick. He made the blind to see and raised the dead back to life. He spoke to the wind and the waves of the sea, and they obeyed Him.

These wonderful works and miracles of Jesus showed the power of God *and* showed His great love for the people. But they did not bring them from death to life. The only way to bring life to the people was for God's Spirit to once again live inside of them.

The Rescue

In the beginning, God said that sin would cause the people to die. Since then, every person who had ever lived had sinned.

The only way for anyone to be rescued from this death was if someone else would die in their place. But there was no one to take their place because there was no one in all of the world who had never sinned.

No one until now - because Jesus had never disobeyed God.

And so, because of His great love for His people, Jesus took the blame for every evil thing they had ever done and every evil thing that they would *ever* do as if He had done these things Himself. He let the people that needed to be rescued nail Him to a wooden cross to die in their place.

We cannot even imagine the horrible pain Jesus felt on that cross or the great sorrow that came upon Him by carrying the guilt of all of the world's sin.

Jesus could have made it all stop, but He did not. He would do all that His Father asked Him to do. This was God's plan to rescue His people and it was why He had come to the world.

And so, Jesus died the death that people had known since that first sin in the garden. His body was put in a dark cave and a large stone was rolled up to close up the *only* way in – *and* the only way out.

But God, who has given life to every person who has ever lived, also has *all power* over death.

And so, God raised His Son, Jesus, from the dead and gave life to Him again! Yes! *Jesus rose up and left that place of death!*

When Jesus' friends saw him, they were amazed! *How could this be?* They had seen the lifeless, torn and ragged body of Jesus placed into a tomb. And He had been dead for *three* days.

But it was true!   *Jesus Was Alive!*   The disciples were filled with great joy and wonder. Once again, they talked with Him. They touched Him. They even ate with Him!

Jesus had conquered death and was in His new body - the kind of body that would never die, the kind He would one day give to each of His children.

Now it was time for Jesus to return to Heaven for He had finished all His Father had asked Him to do.

Forty days after Jesus went back to Heaven, His disciples were together talking about all that had happened.

Suddenly, they heard a loud noise coming from Heaven that sounded like a strong wind. They saw something that looked like flames of fire over each person there.

And all at once, they were all filled with God's Spirit! They were alive inside like Adam had been before he sinned. God's Spirit had returned to give them the power to live as God had created them to live. Their dead souls had come to Life!

Then the disciples began to go out and tell others about the mighty deeds of God. They told them that Jesus was the Son of God; that He had died to take the punishment for their sins; and that after three days, God the Father had raised Him from the dead.

Many who heard believed this good news! They turned away from their sin, were baptized, and were given God's Spirit to make them alive inside as God had created them to be. It was a gift from their Heavenly Father.

When we believe that same good news, we receive that same gift. We become God's children. And we call Him, Father.

The Epilogue

Today, God continues to ask people everywhere to believe what Jesus has done for them. And He continues to take care of His children giving them great joy in all things good and working in their lives to make them more like Jesus.

But Satan is still a liar, and He still tempts people to not believe God or obey Him. And when they disobey, they lose some of the good gifts that God wants them to have. As they continue to make their own decisions instead of obeying God, their lives become sad and broken.

Until our bodies die, we will live in this world that has become a battlefield between what is good and what is evil. But God's children can walk fearlessly and with joy even in the battle because our Father has given us the power to overcome what is evil with good.

But the battle will not go on forever. Someday, Jesus will come back and gather His children to be with Him.

And when all who will believe have believed, God will destroy this broken world and create a new one where there will be no evil.

We will have new bodies which will never die. We will see all that we have believed and even more than we can now imagine. And we will live forever with God in His perfect world.

And our rescue will be complete.

"And I heard a loud voice from the throne saying,
Behold, the dwelling place of God is with man.
He will dwell with them and they will be His people,
and God Himself will be with them as their God.
He will wipe away every tear from their eyes,
And death shall be no more,
Neither shall there be mourning,
Nor crying, nor pain anymore,
For the former things have passed away.
And He who was seated on the throne said
'Behold, I am making all things new.'"

Revelation 21:3-5a

www.ingramcontent.com/pod-product-compliance
Lightning Source LLC
LaVergne TN
LVHW072118070426
835510LV00003B/110